HAL•LEONARD
INSTRUMENTAL PLAY-ALONG

AUDIO ACCESS INCLUDED

PLAYBACK+
Speed • Pitch • Balance • Loop

VIOLA

Disney
Beauty AND THE Beast

T0086621

To access audio visit:
www.halleonard.com/mylibrary

Enter Code
8720-4995-0744-1611

ISBN 978-1-4950-9618-1

Wonderland Music Company, Inc.
Walt Disney Music Company

DISTRIBUTED BY

HAL•LEONARD®

7777 W. BLUEMOUND RD. P.O. BOX 13819 MILWAUKEE, WI 53213

In Australia Contact:
Hal Leonard Australia Pty. Ltd.
4 Lentara Court
Cheltenham, Victoria, 3192 Australia
Email: ausadmin@halleonard.com.au

Visit Hal Leonard Online at
www.halleonard.com

ARIA

VIOLA

Music by ALAN MENKEN
Lyrics by TIM RICE

BE OUR GUEST

VIOLA

Music by ALAN MENKEN
Lyrics by HOWARD ASHMAN

BEAUTY AND THE BEAST

VIOLA

Music by ALAN MENKEN
Lyrics by HOWARD ASHMAN

BELLE

VIOLA

Music by ALAN MENKEN
Lyrics by HOWARD ASHMAN

DAYS IN THE SUN

VIOLA

Music by ALAN MENKEN
Lyrics by TIM RICE

EVERMORE

VIOLA

Music by ALAN MENKEN
Lyrics by TIM RICE

GASTON

VIOLA

Music by ALAN MENKEN
Lyrics by HOWARD ASHMAN

HOW DOES A MOMENT LAST FOREVER

VIOLA

Music by ALAN MENKEN
Lyrics by TIM RICE

THE MOB SONG

VIOLA

Music by ALAN MENKEN
Lyrics by HOWARD ASHMAN

SOMETHING THERE

VIOLA

Music by ALAN MENKEN
Lyrics by HOWARD ASHMAN